Homes
AROUND
the WORLD

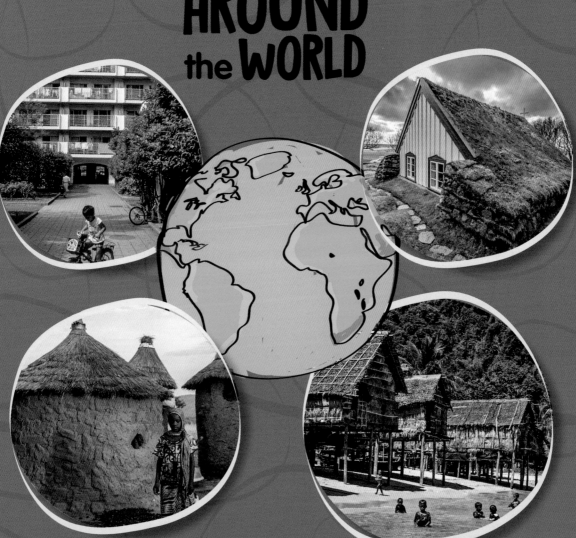

by Lisa M. Herrington

Children's Press®
An imprint of Scholastic Inc.

Library of Congress Cataloging-in-Publication Data
Names: Herrington, Lisa M., author.
Title: Homes around the world/Lisa M. Herrington.
Description: First edition. | New York: Children's Press, an imprint of Scholastic Inc., 2021. |
   Series: Around the world | Includes index. | Audience: Ages 5–7. | Audience: Grades K–1. |
   Summary: "This book shows the many ways people live around the world"— Provided
   by publisher.
Identifiers: LCCN 2021000144 (print) | LCCN 2021000145 (ebook) | ISBN 9781338768640 (library binding) |
   ISBN 9781338768657 (paperback) | ISBN 9781338768664 (ebook)
Subjects: LCSH: Dwellings—Juvenile literature. | Dwellings—Cross–cultural studies—Juvenile literature. |
   Housing—Juvenile literature.
Classification: LCC GT172 .H477 2021 (print) | LCC GT172 (ebook) | DDC 392.3/6—dc23
LC record available at https://lccn.loc.gov/2021000144
LC ebook record available at https://lccn.loc.gov/2021000145

Copyright © 2022 by Scholastic Inc.

All rights reserved. Published by Children's Press, an imprint of Scholastic Inc., *Publishers since 1920*. SCHOLASTIC, CHILDREN'S PRESS, AROUND THE WORLD™, and associated logos are trademarks and/or registered trademarks of Scholastic Inc.

The publisher does not have any control over and does not assume any responsibility for author or third-party websites or their content.

No part of this publication may be reproduced, stored in a retrieval system, or transmitted in any form or by any means, electronic, mechanical, photocopying, recording, or otherwise, without written permission of the publisher. For information regarding permission, write to Scholastic Inc., Attention: Permissions Department, 557 Broadway, New York, NY 10012.

10 9 8 7 6 5 4 3 2 1   22 23 24 25 26

Printed in Heshan, China 62
First edition, 2022

Series produced by Spooky Cheetah Press
Cover and book design by Kimberly Shake

Photos ©: cover top left, 1 top left: Nomad Picturemakers/Getty Images; cover top right, 1 top right: Rui Baiao/Dreamstime; cover bottom left, 1 bottom left: Denis-Huot Michel/age fotostock; cover bottom right, 1 bottom right: Craig Lovell/Education Images/Universal Images Group/Getty Images; 4 left: Geography Photos/Universal Images Group/Getty Images; 4 center: FOTOGRAFIA INC/Getty Images; 4 right: GeoPic/Alamy Images; 5 left: Purestock/Alamy Images; 5 right: Nikolay Antonov/Dreamstime; 6: Aleksandr Faustov/Dreamstime; 7: Edmund Sumner/View Pictures/Universal Images Group/Getty Images; 8: jax10289/Getty Images; 9: JenniferPhotographyImaging/Getty Images; 11: Grant Faint/Getty Images; 12: Evgeniy Fesenko/Dreamstime; 14: Denis Huot Michel/age fotostock; 16: John Elk III/Getty Images; 18: Nancy Brown/Getty Images; 19: Suriyapong Thongsawang/Getty Images; 20: Max Maximov Photography/Dreamstime; 24: Ren_Timmermans/VW Pics/Universal Images Group/Getty Images; 25: Stefano Ember/Dreamstime; 26-27 background: Jim McMahon/Mapman ®; 26 top: Steve Proehl/Getty Images; 26 bottom: Diego Grandi/Dreamstime; 27 top: Stevanzz/Dreamstime; 27 center: Marc Dozier/Getty Images; 27 bottom: Images/AGF/Universal Images Group/Getty Images; 28 center: Ritu Jethani/Dreamstime; 28 right: Jago Jan Veith; 29 top: Atlantide Phototravel/Getty Images; 29 bottom left: Mistervlad/Dreamstime; 29 bottom center: Frans Lemmens/Getty Images; 29 bottom right: byakkaya/Getty Images; 31: Nancy Brown/Getty Images.

All other photos © Shutterstock.

TABLE of CONTENTS

introduction
JUST LIKE ME

Kids in every country around the world have a lot in common. They go to school and play. They have families and friends. Still, some things—like where they call home—can be very different!

POLAND

CUBA

NEPAL

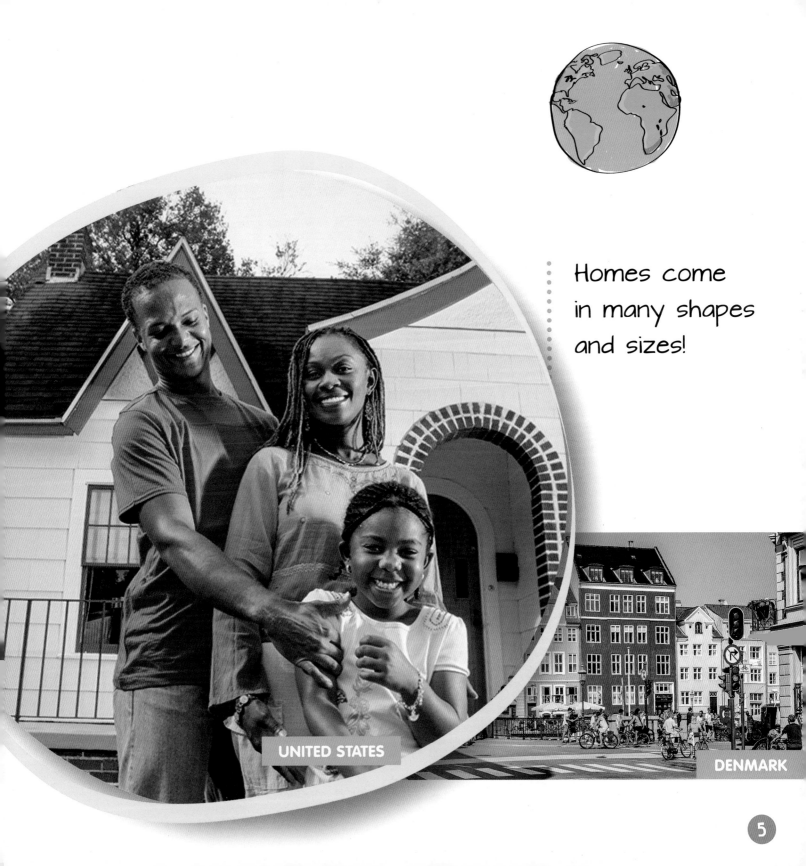

Homes come in many shapes and sizes!

UNITED STATES

DENMARK

chapter 1
FROM CITY TO COUNTRY

There are many kinds of homes around the world. Some people live in tall **apartment** buildings. These buildings can be found in busy cities, such as Tokyo, Japan. Row houses are common in London. That is a big city in England. Row houses are joined side by side.

Some row houses have apartments inside. In England, apartments are called flats.

There are many apartments on each floor of an apartment building like this one in Japan.

A bungalow usually has a porch. The porch helps keep the small house cool.

Many homes are found in neighborhoods outside cities. Some people in Australia live in small houses called **bungalows**. **Farmhouses** can be found in some parts of the United States. In Iowa, for example, about 90 percent of the land is used for farming. Farmhouses are located on land with fields for animals or crops.

People who live in farmhouses often have separate barns.

chapter 2

BUILDING MATERIALS

Homes are built differently depending on their location. In some places, they are built to keep out the cold. People in Iceland once lived in wooden turf houses. Grass and soil covered the house. That held in the heat. Wooden chalets in the mountains of Switzerland have sloped roofs. Snow can slide right off!

A lot of snow falls on the mountains in Switzerland!

People lived in Iceland's turf houses until the 1960s.

Some people in warm places live in **adobe** homes. These homes are made of mud and clay that has been dried into brick. Adobe bricks keep the inside of the house cool. Adobe houses are common in Iran and the southwestern United States. The Taos Pueblo people of New Mexico have lived in multistory adobe buildings for more than 1,000 years.

This adobe village is one of the oldest in Iran.

Sometimes people use ladders to reach the upper floors of an adobe home.

13

Thatched roofs help keep rain out.

14

Many people build their homes using natural materials found nearby. Sticks and mud are often used to build **huts** in African villages. In Burkina Faso, many huts have **thatched** roofs made of grasses. In Sri Lanka, some people use palm leaves to make parts of their homes.

Sticks and leaves from palm trees were used to make this hut in Sri Lanka.

15

chapter 3

HOMES FOR ALL LIFESTYLES

Some homes have a lot of history. Long ago, homes on Santorini island in Greece were built very close together. This was to protect the village from pirates! Some houses in Indonesia look like boats. Many people think the shape shows how people first traveled to that place.

These wooden boat-shaped homes in Indonesia are called *tongkonan*.

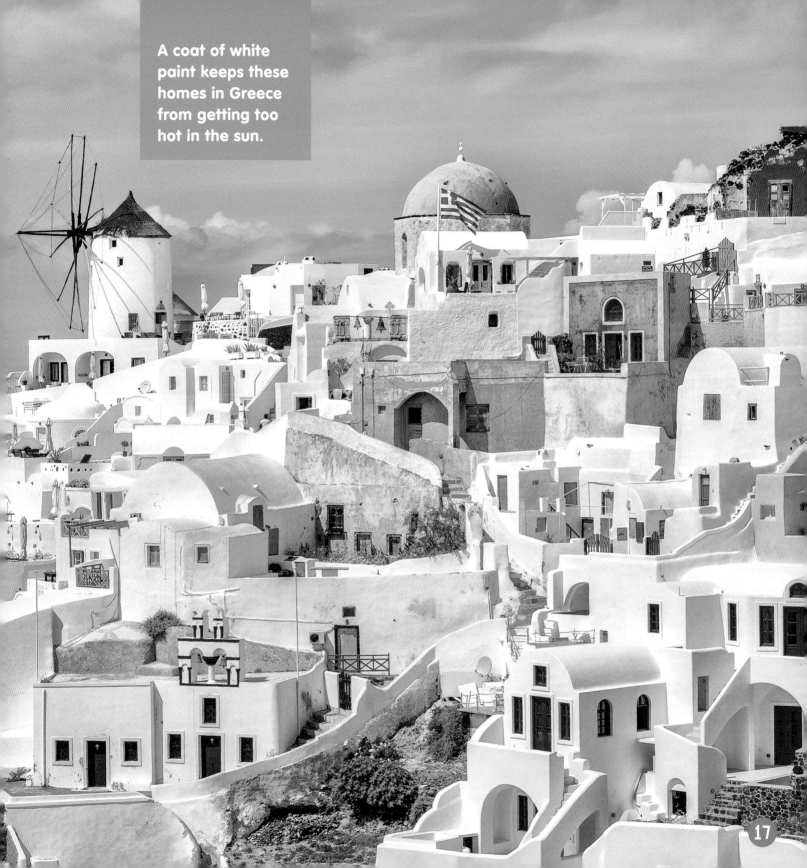

A coat of white paint keeps these homes in Greece from getting too hot in the sun.

17

A ger can take up to three hours to set up or take down.

Some people move with their homes! For thousands of years, **herders** in Mongolia have lived in round tents called **gers**. They travel with farm animals that need land to graze. The herders can take down their tents and build them somewhere else. In New Zealand, about 8,000 people live in motor homes. They can drive to a new area anytime they want!

People can explore New Zealand's beautiful landscape from their motor homes.

chapter 4
WATER WORLD

Many homes around the world are found near oceans, rivers, and lakes. In Thailand, some homes sit high on poles called stilts to keep water out. The water flows under the house rather than into it. In some villages in Chile, people can fish right from their homes.

These colorful stilt homes in Chile are known as *palafitos*.

People often build stilt homes in places like Thailand that get a lot of rain and may be flooded.

Some people around the world live right on the water—in floating villages! In Peru, the Uros people live on floating islands made of grasslike plants called reeds. Their homes and boats are built of reeds, too. In Vietnam, wooden houses make up floating fishing villages.

Children who live on Peru's Lake Titicaca often learn to swim before they walk.

Kids who live in this fishing village in Vietnam go to a school that floats on water!

23

About 2,500 houseboats line the waterways in Amsterdam, the capital of the Netherlands.

In Amsterdam, people live in **houseboats** that float in place. Nearly all houseboats in Kashmir, India, stay in place, too. Most of their owners make their living by fishing.

You have explored many kinds of homes, from houseboats to high-rise apartment buildings. What is your home like?

Some people in India rent out their houseboats to **tourists**.

IF YOU LIVED HERE . . .

Let's look at more interesting homes around the world!

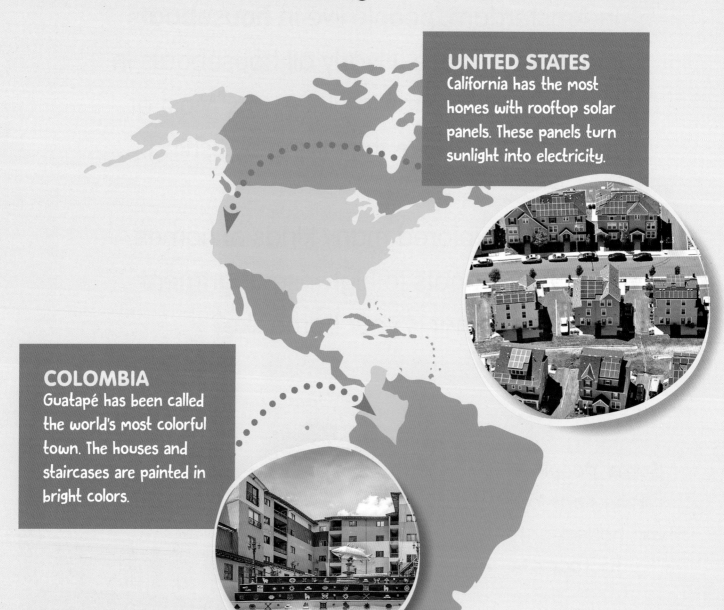

UNITED STATES
California has the most homes with rooftop solar panels. These panels turn sunlight into electricity.

COLOMBIA
Guatapé has been called the world's most colorful town. The houses and staircases are painted in bright colors.

ITALY

An area called Apulia in southern Italy is famous for its trulli homes. They look like something out of a fairy tale with their cone-shaped roofs.

AUSTRALIA

Coober Pedy is a mining town in the Great Victoria Desert. Many people there live in underground homes called dugouts.

SOUTH AFRICA

Ndebele women paint their homes in a traditional style of African art.

A CLOSER LOOK

From castles to caves, there are many unusual homes around the world.

England

Windsor Castle has been the home of kings and queens for about 1,000 years. It is the oldest and largest lived-in castle in the world.

United States

The Glass House in New Canaan, Connecticut, is now a museum. But it was once home to the architect who designed it.

Costa Rica

Most tree houses are used for play or adventure. But some people go out on a limb and live in or rent these high-up homes in the trees.

A girl relaxes in her underground room in Tunisia.

Austria

The Hundertwasser House in Vienna draws visitors from around the world. The colorful apartment building has a rooftop garden.

Tunisia

These underground homes protect against the desert heat and wind. One was even used as Luke Skywalker's home on Tatooine in *Star Wars*.

Turkey

These cave homes in Cappadocia were carved out of rock. Their pointed shapes were formed from volcanic eruptions long ago.

GLOSSARY

adobe (uh-DOH-bee) bricks made of clay mixed with straw and dried in the sun

apartment (uh-PAHRT-muhnt) a set of rooms to live in, usually on one floor of a building

bungalows (BUHNG-guh-lohz) small houses, usually with only one floor

farmhouses (FAHRM-hous-ez) homes on land used to grow crops and raise animals

gers (GAIRZ) round tents that can be moved

herders (HURD-erz) people who move animals together in a group

houseboats (HOUS-bohts) boats that people live on, with places for cooking and sleeping

huts (HUHTS) small, very simple houses

thatched (THACHT) made from dried plants, such as straw or reeds

tourists (TOOR-ists) people who travel and visit places for pleasure

INDEX

ABOUT THE AUTHOR

Lisa M. Herrington can often be found in her cozy home writing books for kids. She is the author of more than 60 of them! Herrington lives in Trumbull, Connecticut, with her husband and daughter. Wherever she is with them, she feels right at home.